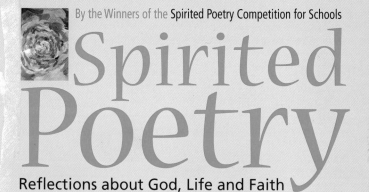

By the Winners of the Spirited Poetry Competition for Schools

Spirited
Poetry

Reflections about God, Life and Faith

Edited by **Lat Blaylock**

for

PCfRE, The National Association for Teachers of RE

RMEP

RELIGIOUS AN

D1151389

Religious and Moral Education Press
A division of SCM-Canterbury Press Ltd
A wholly owned subsidary of Hymns Ancient & Modern Ltd
St Mary's Works, St Mary's Plain
Norwich, Norfolk NR3 3BH

First published 2006

ISBN 978 1 85175 348 2 (book only)
ISBN 978 1 85175 349 9 (book and CD-ROM)

Acknowledgements
This collection of spirited poetry is edited from the competition entries of the same name by Lat Blaylock of PCFRE / RE Today.

I should like to thank my fellow judges, Penelope Wilcock and Lesley Prior for their wonderful insight, enthusiasm and expertise in this project.

PCfRE is grateful to the St Peter's Saltley Trust for their sponsorship of the competition.

We especially thank the hundreds of teachers who gave their time, energy and creative efforts to inspire classes of children to take part in Spirited Poetry.

Last and most, we wish to thank every single pupil who entered the competition, from age 5–19, for all their inspiration, spirituality, effort and care.

Designed and typeset by TOPICS – The Creative Partnership, Exeter

Illustrations by winners of PCfRE's Spirited Arts Competition for Schools

Printed in Great Britain by Halstan and Co. Ltd, Amersham, Buckinghamshire for SCM-Canterbury Press Ltd, Norwich

Contents

Life's like ...   Is life like a puzzle, a journey, a rat   9
race, a disease, a gift of God or a
poisoned chalice? The poems on this
theme look at life from many angles.

Faith   Who do you trust? Where do you put   27
your faith? In these poems the writers
reflect on their own issues and ideas
about trust and faith – in God, or in
humanity.

I wonder ...   Where are we from, where are we   57
going, what are we worth and who
can prove it? All the questions and all
the replies are the wide territory for
this theme.

Where is God?   Atheists say God's nowhere. Agnostics   85
think he may be hiding. Feminists
think he's a she. Believers may place
the divine in the human heart, in the
sacred space, in the running waves or
in deep space. Many different points
of view are represented here.

Introduction

Spirited poetry is the poetry that tussles with the big questions of life, kicks at the darkness or celebrates the verve of living. Spirited poetry asks awkward questions, dreams impossible dreams and yells angry thoughts. It sometimes rests easy in tranquil mood and sometimes it agitates. Atheists and agnostics can write spirited poetry just as well as Muslims, Christians or Hindus.

This anthology of children's and young people's spirited poetry includes over 100 poems written for the Professional Council for RE's competition 'Spirited Poetry'. The competition, run nationally in Winter 2005, attracted many hundreds of wonderful entries from across the 5–18 age range. PCfRE, the subject teachers association for RE, promotes creativity and imagination in RE and teachers of RE all over the country got their teeth into our four themes, enabling pupils to write some stunning stuff. We are grateful to the St Peter's Saltley Trust for their generous sponsorship of the competition.

The competition was judged by Penelope Wilcock (published poet and Christian minister), Lesley Prior (RE teacher trainer and adviser) and Lat Blaylock (PCfRE Executive member and editor of *RE Today*). Winners were selected across the age range, and the poems in this anthology were chosen. Many other wonderful poems have been left out for reasons of space: the standard of entries was very high indeed.

In judging the poetry we were especially looking for spiritual depth, excellence in the use of language and an authentic voice from the entrants. We found all these in abundance, as the pages that follow show. The pupil's voice in education is sometimes stereotyped as negative, bored or disaffected. These pupils' voices are thoughtful, profound, sometimes witty, always alert to the spirituality of life.

Spirited Poetry CD-ROM

An edition of this book is available with a CD-ROM for teachers: ISBN 978-1-85175-349-9. The CD contains:

- All poems and illustrations in the book
- Notes on each of the poems
- Twelve strategies for using poetry for good RE or a good assembly. Each strategy is suitable for primary or secondary pupils and is illustrated with examples referring to poems in *Spirited Poetry*.

Winners of the competition:

Winning entrant	Poem title and page	School	Age
James Ponting	Life is like the sea, p.10	Oldbury on Severn CE Primary School	7
Joseph Sibley	Will there be a third world war? p.59	St Cuthbert's CE Primary School	7
Nicholas Martin	God is everywhere, p.87	Manston St James CE Primary School	8
Dominic Halter	Beware Goliath comes, p.32	St Peter's Primary School, Nottinghamshire	10
Peter Blowfield	Heaven, p.64	Stephen Freeman School, Didcot	10
Max Cobb	Faith: the gates of grace, p.35	Abingdon School, Oxfordshire	11
Thomas White	Apple of Eden, p.98	Lucton School, Herefordshire	11
Casper van der Sman	Spirits, p.36	Graveney School, Tooting	12
Isabelle-Rose Tulloch	The slaves and I, p.38	Kingsbury School, Birmingham	12
Jayne Perks	I am God, p.101	Lacan Childe School, Shropshire	13
Daisy Johnson	Prayer of a dying atheist, p.106	Friends School, Saffron Walden	14
Nadia Al Refaie	I wonder why we breathe, p.80	Leventhorpe School, Hertfordshire	14
Kate Turner	Life's drama, p.26	William Allitt School, Derbyshire	14
Becky Bennett	When the morning bird cries, p.104	Wallingford School, Oxfordshire	14
Jon Ord	Where is God? I've got him, p.112	Ashington School, Northumberland	16
Georgie Shipp	Deep, p.83	Oaklands Catholic School, Hertfordshire	17
Laura Tully	Disguised, p.84	Ashington School, Northumberland	17

Judges: Penelope Wilcock, published poet. Lesley Prior, RE lecturer at the London Institute of Education and chair of the Shap Working Party on World Religions in Education. Lat Blaylock, editor of *RE Today* and PCfRE project worker.

"The judges' task was difficult because the quality of entries was high and impressive. We looked for originality, insight and good use of language in the interpretation of the theme pupils made. We wish to thank all teachers who enabled pupils to take part as well as the pupils: judging spirited poetry has been a wonderful experience."

Poems and contributors

Life's like

Faith

I wonder

Where is God?

Schools

The schools whose pupils wrote poems published in this book include:

Abbey CE VA Primary School; Abingdon School; Acton Park Junior School; Ailwyn School; Arborfield CE Junior School; Ashington Community High School; Blackheath High School; Boxgrove Primary School; Brine Leas High School; Burton End County Primary School; Cheadle Primary School; Clayton Hall School; Coleshill CE Infant School; Cradley CE Primary School; Dame Allen's School; Eaton Square School; English Martyrs RC School, Leicester; Farnborough Grange Infant School; Furzedown Primary School; Graveney School, Tooting; Hesketh Fletcher CE School; King Edward VI High School for Girls, Birmingham; Kingsbury School; Kingstone School; Lacon Childe School; Leventhorpe School; Limehurst High School; London Nautical School; Lucton School; Malden High School; Manston St James School; Meanwood Primary School; Mill Hill School; Mill Vale School; Nancledra County Primary School; Normanhurst School; Norwood Green Primary School; Oaklands Catholic School; Oldbury on Severn Primary School; Parkwood Infants School, Scunthorpe; Pelynt School; Plodder Lane School; Plymouth College; Prior Park School, Bath; Queen Elizabeth Hospital School, Bristol; Selby High School; Shibden Head Primary School; St Chad's Catholic High School, Cheshire; St Cuthbert's CE Primary School, Leicestershire; St Lawrence RC Primary School, Feltham; St Patrick's RC Primary School, Stockton; St Peter's Primary School, West Bridgeford; St Phillip's CE Primary School, Bradford; St Thomas More Catholic Primary School, Leicester; Stanwell School; Stephen Freeman School; Stratford High School; Friends' School, Saffron Walden; Thomas Hardye School; William Allitt School, Derbyshire; Wallingford School; Wallington County Grammar School.

Illustrations

The illustrations in this book are by entrants in the third (2005) Spirited Arts competition organised by the Professional Council for Religious Education. For more information, visit www.pcfre.org.uk/spiritedarts

The schools whose pupils created these illustrations include:

Bluecoat School, Oldham; Folkestone School for Girls; Friends School, Saffron Walden; Harlaw Academy, Aberdeen; Haymoor Middle School, Poole; Holden Clough Primary School, Tameside; Kesteven & Sleaford High School; Notre Dame High School, Sheffield; Priory School, Slough; Springfield School, Portsmouth; St John the Baptist CE Primary School, Bromley; St Mary's Primary School, Putney; St Thomas More Catholic Primary School, Leicester; Wallingford School.

Find Your Own Path
Sakshi Sircar, Age 16

Life's like

Looking at life is a popular activity: is life like a puzzle, a journey, a rat race, a disease, a gift of God or a poisoned chalice?

This theme invited pupils to look at life from any angle they liked, making metaphors and symbols. Among the many excellent entries, children and young people who developed a metaphor in fresh and personal ways were common.

Life
Emma Handley, Age 6

Life is like a box of chocolates,
You never know what you're going to get.

Life is like a jack in a box,
You never know when it will pop out.

Life is like a snail,
You never know what is going on inside its shell.

Life is like a prayer,
You never know what it is going to say.

Life is like a new car,
You never know what it's going to look like.

Now which chocolate shall I pick?

Life is like the sea
James Ponting, Age 7

Life is like the sea
It is calm
It is strong
It is dangerous
It has dangerous animals
It is scary
It is gentle
It is peaceful
I like Life

I like life
Charlie Wilson, Age 7

I like Life because …
It is not dull and black
Life is like my imagination
Life is a miracle
Life is a stunning thing
There are oceans so blue
With oceans critters
I like Life.

Life is like …
Eibhlin Kissack, Age 9

Life's like a well,
You fall down
and get picked up again
in God's hands.
Life's like an award,
You have your moment to shine.
Life's like a pencil box,
It has all the beautiful colours in it.
Life's like a garden,
It grows in tender care.
Life's like a rubber,
You can rub out the horrible parts.
Life's like a river,
It's ever, ever flowing.

Life is like a lift
Charlie Boyd, Age 7

Life is like a lift
Ding ding level one: learning to walk
Ding ding level two: learning to talk
Ding ding level three: going to school
Ding ding level four: swimming in a pool.
People getting in, people getting out,
Life is like a lift
That's all it's about.

Life's like soup
Rebekah Connor, Age 11

Life's like a big pot of soup,
The vegetables, humans.
The sauce, the lakes and seas,
The potatoes, classed as land.

All mixed together,
To make God's favourite recipe.
To make life and death,
To make friends and enemies.

Then finally God's last touch,
To stir the soup of life.
To eventually make man,
Live how God has commanded.

Walk in His Steps
Abby Fox, Age 11

Life's like a rainbow
Aiesha Kinnear, Age 10

Some days I feel blue.
I am feeling sad.
Do you feel it too?

Yesterday I felt red.
I was angry at something you did
Or something you said.

The times I hear bad news I am black.
I feel all alone
Even if everyone is with me at home.

Sometimes I am envious.
I am green when my brother's getting attention
I just want to be seen.

When something disastrous
Happens in the world I feel white.
I'm confused
And I don't know how to make things right.

When I am scared or frightened
It is a purple day.
The feeling crawls through me
In a slow scary way.

Happy days to me are yellow,
These are the days I feel
So warm, cosy and mellow.

Outside it is raining and so grey.
I am feeling miserable
This is my colour today.

But tonight I'll feel squidgy and pink with love,
When my mum wraps her arms around me
Like the softest glove

Orange is my favourite colour.
This is the colour I feel
When I know God is with me.
No matter how I was feeling before
This is the best one,
Don't you agree?

The advantages of mistakes
Marie Grace Genova, Age 13

Every move we make
Is a mistake

Like a painter
Use the brush you were given
And paint
To create your masterpieces
Life

Listen to
Your breath
Your heartbeat
What colours?
What shapes?
Designs?

Life is your mistake
Make mistakes
Blobs
Misdirected strokes

Beauty

Life's like a flowerbed
Rhiannon Owen, Age 13

… A flowerbed.
Not a bed of roses,
Just a flowerbed.

Not that pretty,
A work in progress,
Still full of weeds.

Waiting for a gardener,
To play God,
Pull out the bad bits
Leaving the good.

But which bits do you take,
From the flowerbeds of life?
Is it the death & dying?

The pain, the crying?
Is the day worth finishing
Or is it just life?

Does life need to be scarred,
By the dandelions and nettles,
Which haunt this life?

But then I think:
Does this make me
The person I am
Today?

Life's like a walnut
Amy Evans, Age 13

Life's like a walnut,
you can only get out
once you're open enough to enter reality.
"Roll up, roll up come and join the rat race"

The train of existence paces on and on.
Innovation and renovation starts here and ends at the red light.
Your head spins and your stomach turns,
Your heart thuds and your feet stand still,
And then you move.

And there are questions and answers,
Why are we here?
What is non-existence?
And if it exists, where do we go?

Problems break you they snap you
And laughter is like a plaster
A giant healer sent by god
Faith is strong but trust is unbeatable
Life's like a giant headache,
While you're taking a paracetamol
Doses lightly waver the world
Pain, no pain, pain, no pain
Pain, no pain, pain, no pain

And then the red light appears
We go through the tunnel
And then …
Non-existence

Life
Alex Gant, Age 13

Life is like a mystery,
No one knows its depths.
Life is like a roller coaster,
It takes turns right and left.

I wonder what life is like,
No one really knows.
No one knows where it really starts,
Or even where it goes.

Faith is like music,
It has its different views.
Faith contains no right or wrong,
You cannot win or lose.

"Where is God?" the whole world asks,
Is he real or not?
Is the God a he or a she?
This question's asked a lot.

Life is like a butterfly,
It is enriched with beauty.
Life's been made to make you happy
That's its real duty.

Inspiration: Mosque, Temple, Sky
Olivia Jarman, Age 14

That's life
Polly Holton, Age 13

Life's like the first cry of a baby,
Such joy, but over so quickly

Life's like the dreams of millions
Wanting to be something,
But never will be

Life's like peace in the world,
An idea, an ideal, but misused

Life's like climbing a mountain,
Hard work just for a memory

Life's like a memory,
So much better when you look back

Life's like a journey,
The excitement of an expectation but never getting there

Life's like a story,
Passed down through generations, and changed every time

Life's like waiting for Christmas
But you never get what you wanted
If life was like this, then why would we live?
Life isn't a definition, it's just what it is.

Life is like a river
Lizzy Pitts & Lauren Flaherty, Age 16

Plop!
That's it.
This is where it all begins.
To begin with,
Steady movement,
Meandering around rocks, reeds, rubble;
Gradually gaining momentum,
Starting to speed round bends like Schumacher,
Through the rough rapids,
Like a whirlwind,
Everything rushing around;
Then, suddenly …
Silence, tranquillity.
The smooth journey begins,
Towards that Big Wide World.
Plop!
That's it.
This is you.
One small drop in the open ocean.

Life's like music
Matthew Woodcock, Age 13

Life
One melody
We must play
Until it fades away
And then inevitably
We all
Die

Birth
A symphony
Of great happiness
A new small instrumentalist
Brought into the
Harmony of
Life

Death
The end
Of a piece
By the conductor: God
That ends with
The final
silence

Imagine yourself a bird
Graham Topham, Age 13

Imagine yourself,
A bird of grace,
Born, small and fluffy,
Into a harsh, cruel world.
At first your parents help you;
Teaching you the basics,
Then you're on your own,
Fending for yourself.

The world can teach you everything,
You learn fast,
Quickly in the ways of life,
Slowly in more complex matters.
But everything learnt is an achievement,
An added feather to your fluffy body,
A feather that accumulates,
Every day.

Years go by,
You get stronger, taller,
More headstrong and bold,
Nearing the edge of your perch.
Your feathers are complete,
With the lessons in life,
Worn proudly on your figure,
You stretch your wings and fly.

More is added to foundation feathers,
Flying gets easier through gained confidence.
Though wind and rain may hold flight back,
With hard work you'll prevail,
And fly, beautiful, majestic.
That is what life is like

Life is like a penguin
Victoria Warren, Age 13

Life is like a penguin in many ways and means,
From seeing pretty things to smelling danger on the breeze,
From floating in the sea, to playing in the snow,
From hunger, death and suffering to learning things you've got
      to know.

By its father's feet a baby penguin huddles close,
The mother penguin returns bringing food for them both.
And when the time is right, the baby penguin leaves,
To live an adult life on the ice and in the seas.

Penguins all share special bonds; they know which chick is theirs,
They leave their children in a crèche, whilst fishing for their
      shares.
Penguins mate for life, just like humans do,
They like to gather in crowds called troops;
It's safer with more than two.

A penguin travels slowly north to summer feeding grounds,
In humans this is similar, but it isn't so profound.
In summer many travel to a country far away,
In search of peace and quiet, an exotic holiday.

A penguin cannot always see which way it wants to go,
It can swim into danger, and often this is so.
On the ice there are seals and things which chase and bite,
And in the seas there are sharks and whales, black as night.

Some in both species do not make it;
their fight does not prevail,
They are extinguished by predators, be it lion, shark or whale.
Both species have a place that they feel safe to call their own:

For penguins it's the ice, for humans it's their home.
So life is like a penguin in many different ways,
From families and friendships to danger in the waves.
But one thing which is certain, through trouble, greed and strife,
Both humans and these flightless birds all have the gift of life.

Life's drama
Kate Turner, Age 14

The spotlight switches on
The rest is dark
Nothing else matters
Nothing except you
Then your spotlight fades
Not much, but enough
Others join yours
And light is shared out
Friends join your spotlight
The stage lights appear
They guide you on your path
Round the twists and turns
That tell your life story
People all have a part in your play
Some come and hide behind their masks
They're so convincing
But near the end the masks come off
And you see their true colours
Another spotlight appears
It's your true love
You join and are happy for many scenes
Small spotlights now join you; children
Some scenes later
The spotlight disappears. Darkness
Fast, unfair and cruel

Parting the Red Sea
Jack Hafeez, Age 10

Faith

Noah trusted the promise of the rainbow. Prophet Muhammad (pbuh) trusted the voice of Angel Jibril. Who do you trust? Where do you put your faith?

This theme invited pupils to reflect on their own issues and ideas about trust and faith – in God, or in humanity. Among the many fine entries, some reflected on stories from scriptures or other religious sources, others on the idea of trust, or placing your faith in religion or in God.

27

I have faith
Fay Toms, Age 9

I have faith in my teacher
because I feel safe inside my classroom.
I have faith in my friends
because they never let me down.
I have faith in the vicar
because she is the best vicar and would never shout.
I have faith in the police
because they will try and find your mum or dad if you're lost.
I have faith in my mum and dad
because they love me.
I have faith in my doctor
because he would never hurt me.
I have faith in my family
because they make me happy when I'm sad.
I have faith in the fire fighter
because they would put the fire out.
I have faith in all of these things
because they keep me safe.

Come to us God
Nicola Eames, Age 10

Come to us God
Destroy our hearts of stone
Come to us God
Give us hearts of pure love
Come to us God
In caring and trust
Come to us God
With health and good cheer
Come to us God
In faith and in love
Come to us God

Jesus and the Children
Georgina, Age 14

A Joseph rap
Lauren Duffy & Hannah Spicer, Age 10

My name is Joseph
I am my father's favourite.
I was brought up by four women
And I have eleven brothers.

My brothers don't like me,
Because I'm a Daddy's boy.
I guess it's because they're jealous
But they want to kill me.

They took me to the well
and nearly dropped me down the hole.
They took my favourite coat off me
Then stained it with blood.
They went and told my father
That I was dead.

I wasn't really dead,
I was sold as a slave
To a man called Potiphar.
He took me over to Egypt
And because they were pleased with me
They put me in charge of his household.

His wife was very pleased with me,
She loved me
But I didn't love her.
She accused me of attacking her
As the lies spilled from her mouth.

But now I am:
Good interpreter,
Scared prisoner,

Fabulous adviser,
A second commander,
A long lost brother,
Trickster and traitor,

God's faithful believer!

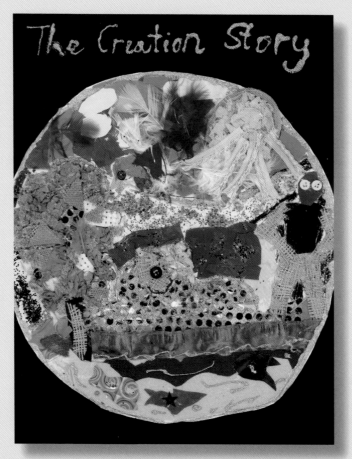

Year 1 Pupils, Priory School, Slough

Beware Goliath comes!
Dominic Halter, Age 10

A wave soars towards the shore,
As colossal as two elephants on the plain,
Tourists rooted to the spot,
Like an iceberg of terror has wrapped itself around them.
Beware Goliath comes!
    Fill your sling with sunshine
    And evaporate their grief.

People sit paralysed,
Having forgotten how to live,
The strength of independence faded,
Their spirits left with the terrible company of loneliness.
Beware Goliath comes!
    Fill your sling with desire
    And bring life.

Minutes fly past,
Hours go by,
Starvation glides through the atmosphere,
Children lie waiting,
Patiently,
Waiting for the taste of death
That swims across the landscape.
Beware Goliath comes!
    Fill your sling with the light of hope
    And let the starving see the silver lining.

Mothers grieve for the loss of their babies,
Children cry over their dead parents,
People fall into the depths of despair,
Tramps find the door of life shut,
Locking them in the room of death.
Beware Goliath comes!
    Fill your sling with people and loved ones
    And bring them back into the joy of our world.

Woodcutters destroying rain forests,
Insects, animals, birds left homeless,
Fleeing from the chainsaw of terror and death.
Falling down like the trees …
Dead!
Beware Goliath comes!
    Fill your sling with compassion and respect
        And bring laughter.

See Goliath fall!

Misery: Elijah taken up to heaven
Abigail Porter, Age 11

I was wrapped up
In my feelings.
The anger,
The pain.

Lying on the cold ground,
Sobbing my tears.
They were still inside.
I could not release them.

There was no hope
As I climbed
With the gazing eyes
Of the young man.

I came to the top,
The light was there.
Angels staring at me.
I knew I was OK.

As I was lifted,
The angels took me.
I threw my cape
And felt my happiness.

Faith: the gates of grace
Max Cobb, Age 11

My weak prayers are not enough to heal
The ancient wounds so deep and so dear
This is the revelation of hatred and fear

What a wicked game to play
To make us feel this way
Are we going to heaven
Or shall we just wait?

So keep on pretending
It will be the end of our craving
Keep on pretending
It's all right

When your passing comes
The game begins
The one we will never win
The only way to heaven

It could be all right
Don't let us grow cold
We pray to him
But does he listen?

Softly the light shines in
Through the gates of grace
On me and you
Deceiving our restless hearts

Stop being what you believe in
And start being who you are.

Spirits

Caspar Jubril van der Sman, Age 12

The spirit of goodness says:
"Rejoice ye peoples
Overlook your differences.
Forget your woes."

The spirit of Godliness says:
"Live in harmony my children
Lead good lives
And God's grace be bestowed on you."

The spirit of science says:
"Do not be blindly led by
Spirituality and its promises
They are all false."

The spirit of humanity says:
"Worry! Stress! These things are your life
Vote and grow
And breed and die."

The spirit of death says:
"Life is but a flicker
Welcome its passing
Into the infinite death."

The spirit of reality says:
"I will kill you all.
I am wealthy and powerful
I run your lives."

The spirit of morbidity says:
"Life is not worth living surely
Better to embrace death
Which I pretend to know."

The spirit of pain says:
"You people are revolting
You think you have it bad
And you spit on those who do."

The spirit of power says:
"Squabble, fight
It makes no difference to me
I run the world."

The spirit of optimism says:
"Surely things will work out
In heaven at least
Things will be peaceful."

The spirit of nirvana sighs:
"I am empty to those
Who believe not. To those who do
You'll have to wait and see."

The spirit of hell says:
"You'll all be under mine own care
Soon enough
You think yourselves pure …"

The spirit of spirits looks down
On the people's beliefs and sighs
Thinks to itself:
"My people have truly created some wonderful things.
If I were to be as heaven to them
It would be a just reward
But can I?
Is there a heaven for me to promise?
Or will they all fall from my grasp
When their lives slip away?"

The slaves and I: a poem for Moses
Isabelle-Rose Tulloch, Age 12

I'm walking down this dusty unknown path
Not knowing which road I should take.
I think,
Should I go left?
Or should I go right?

I have people,
Lives, upon my shoulders
Crying out for help.
It is my duty to help them live
Not to leave them alone, abandoned.

I can trust no one except Aaron
The one who speaks for me, the one whom I will always trust.
And God above us all
The one who gave me this task to take.

But it is the slaves and I who walk on,
It is the slaves and I who take this path
But we are unsure of where we should go
As we have never been here before.

The only thing we can do
Is put trust in each other
To help one another,
As it is the slaves and I who are taking this path.
The path to freedom.

Who do you trust?
Elliot Taylor, Age 11

Do I trust the weatherman?
Or do I trust the sky?
Do I trust my A-Z?
Or do I trust a passer by?

Do I trust a reporter to give me the facts?
Or do I trust the eyewitness who was there?
Do I trust the hairdresser to do what I want?
Or do I trust my Mum to cut my hair?
Do I trust a policeman to tell me the time?
Or do I trust my watch is still working?
Do I trust a doctor who tells me I am better?
Or do I trust my body that says it is still hurting?

Do I trust my brother who says he is a genius?
Or do I trust my knowledge that he is a liar?
Do I trust the smoke alarm that nothing is wrong?
Or do I trust my eyes that tell me the house is on fire?

Do I trust the dentist who says it will not hurt?
Or do I trust my teeth that say they are in pain?
Do I trust the TV advert that says that their soap powder is special?
Or do I trust my Nan who says they are all the same?

Do I trust the instructions for my new computer game?
Or do I trust a friend who says he has played it before?
Do I trust my Dad who says I have eaten enough?
Or do I trust my stomach that says I need more?

Do I trust myself?
I think I do.

I place my faith
Amy Brazil, Age 11

I place my faith in those around me,
Those whom I know.
I place my faith in those I trust,
Who never seem to go.

I place my faith in the clock,
Whose time slowly slips by.
I place my faith in others' wisdom,
And trust them not to lie.

I place my faith in evolution,
The chance to always grow.
I place my faith in others' teachings,
For they always seem to know.

I place my faith in my god,
Who watches over me.
I place my faith in my god,
Who never fails to see.

I place my faith in the plants,
That never fail to grow.
I place my faith in the smile,
That stops me from feeling low.

I place my faith in all that I know,
For it never leaves me alone.
But most of all I place my faith,
In me, and me alone.

Fractured Christ
Jennie Atkinson, Age 15

Allah

Ahmed Kandeel, Age 12

Timeless in motion.
Timeless in space.
Timeless in another dimension.

Where is Allah?
Where are You?
A question perplexing
Since the dawn of time,
The answer?
Closer to me than the veins in my neck.
Our purpose? To worship Allah;
To know Him, to love Him, to obey,
To live life.

Where is Allah?
Where are You?
Timeless and apart,
Apart from time.
For time does not command You.
Only You command time.
Timeless and away.
Timeless in space.

Who is Allah?
Who are You?
Most Gracious, Most Merciful,
The One, The Only.
Our Creator!

Footsteps in faith
Victoria Bion, Age 13

Follow someone's footsteps
Standing in their shoes,
Don't follow anyone's
Whose? Whose?

Follow someone's footsteps
Footprints in the sand,
Leading off to the unknown,
To some distant land.

Follow in the footsteps
Of Martin Luther King,
Help get rid of racism
Peace and wisdom bring.

Follow in the footsteps
Mother Teresa's way,
Heal the world with kindness
Start right now today.

Follow someone's footsteps
Standing on their shoes
Whose footsteps would you follow?
Whose? Whose?

Easter
Edward Llewellin, Age 11

A carpenter to a priest,
A priest to a king.
Always a good man,
Miracles he did bring.

He rode through Jerusalem,
On a grey old donkey,
Jesus was a good man,
Anyone could see.

At the Last Supper
Jesus broke the bread.
"This is my blood, this is my flesh,"
That's what Jesus said.

Jesus was betrayed at the garden,
He was no coward,
"Do not hurt the Romans," he said,
As he was carried off by a guard.

Jesus was given an unfair trial,
And condemned to die!
"How shall we kill him?" asked a guard.
They replied, "Crucify!"

Jesus pulled his heavy cross up the hill,
With a crown of thorn,
Some wept, some cried,
Some would mock and scorn.

Nailed to a cross
Our King has been crucified.
"Forgive them," he said
And then Jesus died.

He was dragged down
And his body was put in a cave,
To free us from our worst sins
His own life he gave.

The next day a woman
Saw that Jesus' corpse had gone.
Then from the empty cave
An angel shone.

"Jesus' body is not here,"
The bright angel said.
"Do not cry. Smile and laugh:
He has risen from the dead!"

Jesus died to free us from our sins,
So every day we can make fresh starts.
Jesus will never die,
He still living, in our hearts.

Crucifixion: A Day to Remember
David Bridgewood, Age 11

Pentecost
William Mee, Age 12

I wait in that room
With nothing to do,
A flash of light,
A power goes through.

Tongues of fire,
Nothing is burning.
I feel the Lord,
A light, a yearning.

I speak new language,
I am preaching,
My mouth is moving,
My words are reaching.
Out.

Pentecost
Kathryn Dunford, Age 13

Faith
Nick Port, Age 13

Faith flows like a cool stream through rocks,
It has many forms like the colours of a rainbow.
It intertwines as ivy on a tree,
Or words in a sentence.
People turn to it in times of need.
When you find it, it hits you like an iron fist into your stomach,
Then the swirling dizziness after.
It is like love; once you feel it you are addicted
To the comfort of being able to rely upon something.
It is a pillow to rest on,
Yet a poisonous snake that will turn on you
Given any chance.

My faith
Rayyan Dewan, Age 14

My words ain't hypocritical
Like everything that's political
I'm the truth, so spiritual.

My Muslim brothers all for one and one for all
But must be off when I hear the call
My prayer is so critical.

The Qur'an, like my poem, so lyrical
Test everything, all of it's empirical
Unlike some, it's no way theoretical.

So many people just talk battle
Making others frightful and fretful
I find it all so irritable

Not a terrorist 'cos I'm fundamental
Like my religion, I'm so peaceful
Don't wanna fight, to be truthful
I'm so busy being faithful.

Finishing up as I drop my pencil
Remember my message:
Muslims are not harmful
Be careful never call us baleful
If anything just Islamical.

Poem to the Hindu God Brahman

I share my life with you

Emma Corney, Age 13

I can feel you all around me,
In the air that I breathe,
In the sun, the sky, the grasses,
And in the life I lead.

I can feel you in my heart,
In my soul, my thoughts and everywhere,
From the moment I am born
And in the life I share.

I know you will protect me,
Lead me on my way,
I know your presence matters
In all I do and say.

I follow your advices,
And take care that I must heed,
To do what really matters,
And take just what I need,

My eyes, they cannot see you,
Invisible that you are,
But I know that I will listen,
And know you are not far.

Lakshmi Over the Houses
Alex Gibbons & Jordan Claydon, Age 10

A reflection for Krishna
Danny Bithell, Age 14

In the clearing where the flautist Krishna plays,
His happy tunes and jokeful ways.
Amongst the women the bangles glow,
To join them as one for ever more.

When they become one a triangle will form,
For ever more set in stone.
The corners are obvious for the most,
For they represent the Father, Son and Holy Ghost.

Angel or mother is dressed in green,
The colour of life and new growth in spring.
The other women dressed in orange and midnight blue,
Sing praise for the mother who breeds new life into you.

The circle or the wheel of life has no beginning and no end,
This circle will never be broken although it twists and bends.
God's love for everyone will hold it together,
For your life on earth and life after, for ever and ever.

A route to tomorrow
Barney Rolph, Age 14

Faith is a rope
Binding you to someone
As strong as your mind
As weak as your doubt
It's a contract of hope
There are no catches
No small print
It's just faith.

Faith is a rope
A noose round the world
A book of evil
A sentence of death
It commands dark armies
A suicidal race
A weapon of mass destruction
This is faith.

Faith is the rope
Tied to the future
Pulling us forward
Making us better
It's a line for our children
A guiding star
A route to follow
Faith is tomorrow.

Rain down faith
Laura May Ralph, Age 14

When the rain starts to pelt
Its metallic grey
I have my faith

When it clings to my skin
And I can't get away
I have my faith

When the bare branched trees
Get a hold of me
And the sky's so black
That I cannot see
I have my faith

It can banish dark
When it glares so bright
When I shout, the twigs twist away in fright
I am standing strong
In my own spotlight
It's just me and faith
And God and light
I am overwhelmed

When you call me up
On my dying day
I'll see your face
And a hazy glow
Will surround the place
Praise you for faith

You raise me up in your purity
You show me crystal clearly
How I should dream to be
Rain down faith
Rain down faith

Lost my faith
Angela Conway, Age 16

I'm sure you'll identify with my account,
When there's something you want it can never be found.
Of course when you don't need it, it's always right there,
It's when you need it most that finding it's rare.

When I found it was gone, I was rather distraught.
And so I sat for a while, and thought.
Where did I last see it? It can't have gone far,
Down the back of the sofa? In the car?

No, not there … but think, they're bound
To have it at the 'lost and found'
But when I asked if they'd seen it, to no avail,
My hopes of ever finding it were starting to fail.

I searched through the shadows and retraced my steps,
From the highest highs to the deepest depths.
I asked my family, I phoned round my friends,
But they hadn't seen it, so I searched again.

When I went home I searched under my bed,
It wasn't there, but I found something else instead.
Covered with dust, on the front was a cross,
On the side, the words 'Holy Bible' embossed.

I opened it up, and to my surprise,
It jumped off the pages, right before my eyes.
And I thought to myself, as I read through the book,
"Funny, faith's always in the last place you look."

Like you...
Asha Patel, Age 17
[I wrote this after visiting Auschwitz with my school.]

I dream about my parents
How we argue and we fight
But also how they're there for me
How together we stay tight

I dream about my sisters
How they scream and shout all day
How we sometimes disagree
How we used to sit and play

I dream about the holidays
What we did, what we'll do
I dream about the future
Where and what and who

Sometimes I'll dream of nothing
Just like others cannot
Sometimes I won't remember the dream
Exactly as it was

I dream about failing
The nearest set of tests
I dream about being famous
And about being the best

I dream to be a singer
Or dancer or teacher
I dream about making money
About making the world fairer

I dream about things like you
The same thoughts run through me
But my biggest dream of all is
To be able to dream these dreams ...
Like you

Adam and Eve: The Next Steps
Roseanna Ball, Age 13

I wonder

Puzzling questions are fertile ground for poetic imagination. Where are we from, where are we going, what are we worth and who can prove it?

All the questions and all the replies are the wide territory for this theme. Many younger children contributed poetry on this theme, and their speculations were often surprising, profound or intriguing. Learning to love the big questions of life is sometimes necessary before any worthwhile answers can be found.

How does the sun come up?
Caitlin Brown, Age 5

How does the sun come up?
How does the sea come to the shore?
How does the snow come?
How do the clouds stay in the sky?

Why do the stars come out?
Kennedy Lamming, Age 6

Why do the stars come out?
Why do we have names?
How far does the sea go?
How does the moon shine?

Why does a wasp sting?
Why is the grass green?
Why can't we fly?
Why are the clouds in the sky?

I wonder how
Madelaine Knowles, Age 6

I wonder how the world is made?
I wonder how the birds fly?
I wonder how we grow?
I wonder what the deepest sea is?
I wonder why teachers are the boss?
I wonder why we die?

I wonder why
Isaac Thomas, Age 6

I wonder why the world was made
I wonder how plants grow
I wonder how God was made
I wonder how horses can jump so high

Will there be a third world war?
Joseph Sibley, Age 7

There have been too many wars.
We don't deserve
The torture of the human race.
Can't we have peace for once
And let the flowers bloom?

We see the men approach coming to kill.
The sound of the enemy's trudging boots.
The children and women squealing and crying.
Our men dying and fighting for our country.
WILL THERE BE A THIRD WORLD WAR?
Of that I am not sure.

Questions: I wonder
Ellice Hardy, Age 8

Q: I wonder why the sky is so high?
A: So the birds don't hit their heads.
Q: I wonder why the earth is round?
A: So God can play ping pong.
Q: I wonder why trees' stems are called trunks?
A: So the elephants aren't lonely.

I don't know
Kathy Bennett, Age 8

I wonder why the world is round
And why it orbits round the Sun?
I wonder why you never fall off
And why gravity pulls you down?
I DON'T KNOW, I DON'T KNOW

I wonder who named all the things
And I wonder how?
I wonder how people knew
And how hard it was?
I DON'T KNOW, I DON'T KNOW

I wonder how the world was made
Oh I wonder how it was done?
I wonder how hard it was to make
And did he use glue and felt?
I DON'T KNOW, I DON'T KNOW

DO YOU?

I don't know, I don't know
Do you know? Do you know?
I can't think, I can't think
I WONDER EVERYTHING

The question maze
Sophia Brousas, Age 9

I wonder how the world was made.
I wonder why the sky is blue.
I wonder if the world's got bigger.
I wonder if God pulls a trigger
To change from light to dark.
Does he have a magic spark?

I wonder if God sees
Every person in the world.
Every boy and every girl.
If so, how?
Can he see us now?
I've been asking these questions
For days and days.
My mind is in
A question maze.

I wonder why nobody knows.
I wonder why nobody goes
To find the reply
To my question "Why?"

I wonder...
Kevin, Age 9

I wonder why people are disabled
I wonder if ghosts are real
I wonder where there is not gravity
I wonder how many people are in this world
I wonder why the sky is blue
I wonder if there are aliens
I wonder how many planets there are
I wonder how clouds float and split
I wonder how many stars there are
I wonder why people are rich
I wonder why adults and children are naughty
I wonder if stars fall or die

What is the meaning of life?
Joel Lucyszyn, Age 9

The meaning of life is that
We can use its green land,
The still water next to the bank,
Feeling the soft air on your cheek
The people can use its greatness.

But what if there is no meaning, there is nothing
Just an illusion that God has made?
What if there is no life?
What if the pain is
The devil sobbing in his grave?
What if the good in my life is an angel laughing?

Heaven
Peter Blowfield, Age 10

Heaven, Heaven, what does it mean?
Is it a giant recycling machine?
People go up, people come down
When people are old
They go through God's machine
That crushes and pounds

But don't be afraid
Of God's machines
Be grateful, be keen
This will not damage the body
But increase the soul
So please don't be scared
About the recycling machine in the sky
Learn about Heaven
And you will fly
(at least you don't have to moan about getting old)

Paradise
Umar, Age 14

I wonder

Searching for my special place
Robin Johnson, Age 10

Where is it? I don't know,
Is it by a fire with a warming glow?
I will search for it while I'm here,
I just hope it will be near.
Is it inside or outside?
My time to look I shall not hide,
Searching for my special place.

Is it a library – my special place?
Or is it beside a big bookcase?
Will it be somewhere I can relax?
Or to go there will I have to pay tax?
Is it inside a cardboard box?
Or in the woods, running from a fox?
Searching for my special place.

Should I look high or should I look low?
Jump in a river with its steady flow?
I still have not found it,
Even though the clock has struck midnight,
I get snug in bed,
Rest my tired head,
I have found my special place.

The meaning of death
Alex Tandy, Age 10

I wonder: what's the meaning of death?
Why do people pass away?
Gently fading into silence
They are silent to this day.

Why is there sound and silence?
The twins to death and life
Resonating through the ages
With the drop of a knife.

Nobody remains here
In the midst of noise and life
But when they fall to silence
Do they suffer any strife?

Will we conquer death itself,
Or will we go on dying?
All across the world today
There are people crying.

The wonders of the mind
Charlotte Cox, Age 10

An illusion of life,
Like a dark tunnel with a light at the end,
Remarks softly,
"Hallowed be thy name."

Frozen breath,
Like a fast flowing river in spring,
Disappears swiftly into the breeze,
Whispering,
"Hallowed be thy name."

Mighty flashes of light,
Like electric waves of seeing and believing,
Scream,
"Hallowed be thy name."

The mystery of Heaven,
Like a board game of skies and sea,
Mutters,
"Hallowed be thy name."

The power of God,
Like a gigantic force of love and hope,
Says aloud,
"Hallowed be thy name."

The power of God,
Like a gigantic force of love and hope,
Says aloud,
"Hallowed be thy name."

Who am I?
Joe McNeil, Age 10

I am my dreams,
My thoughts,
I am the crossfire of creation and evolution.
I am my knowledge, my wisdom, my grief,
Yet my tears turn to steam on my cheeks.
I am my lost soul
Which finds its way back,
I am my cracked heart
Which is whole once again.
I am my conscience, my will,
I am my own enemy.
I am the question,
Yet there is no answer:
"What is the meaning of life?"

What if ...
Nicole Aibbitt, Age 14

If God gives us peace
Why are there wars?
If God gives us freedom
Why are there laws?
If God gives us life
Why is there death?
If God gives us independence
Why is there theft?
If God gives us happiness
Why are we sad?
If God is our father
Why is there Dad?
If God gives us everything
Why do some have nothing?!

Wondering about bird life
Oliver Brookes, Age 11

I wonder what it would be like
To fly like a bird
To soar above the towns, cities and oceans
Flying and touching the stars
To be able to fly away from the cold

I wonder what it would be like
To be a bird
Small and feathered
Webbed feet standing on a rock
On the cliffs looking out to sea
All I eat is fish and crabs
Different

I wonder what it would be like
To touch the clouds
Shout and not be heard
Run my wings through cloud soft and fluffy
Touch the clouds
Sit on the moon

I wonder, I dream
Joanne Stockton, Age 13

I wonder, I dream,
Of times gone past,
Of forgotten memories,
Of thoughts lost fast.

I wonder, I dream,
Of things up above,
Of things down below,
Of hate and love.

Where is God? What is he?
Making life and history,
Male, female, true or fake,
Transparent or opaque.

Where is God? What is she?
Making life and history,
Is there a heaven? What about a hell?
Making stories for us to tell.

Wondering acrostic
Beth Lardner, Age 13

I wonder if God is pleased?

When he looks down he sees,
Only war, pestilence and disease,
Not only demolishing trees,
Destroying lives with ease,
Everything warming even the birds and bees,
Retribution for Pandora's keys?

What kind of times are these?
Here we are on our knees,
Your mercy, show us please.

Where is God?
Matthew Ebbs, Age 15

Wonderful Counsellor.

Mighty God.

Everlasting Father.

Prince of Peace.

And he will be called

And the increase of His government and peace there will be no end

(Isaiah 9:6-7)

I wonder
Emily Grimes, Age 11

I wonder what dark and gloomy creature
Took peace and unity and threw them in the bin?
Who would want to live in a world of dark
When we can just as easily live in the light?

I wonder what would happen
If we stood by each other once in a while?
Would it make any difference,
Or would people still hover and make us fear?
I wonder

I wonder if we asked God for forgiveness
Would he turn on the lights?
Or would he make us live in a pit for ever?
What if we'd never made it dark in the first place?

Agnostic acrostic
Calvin Ross, Age 12

Am not sure about God
Go and find him in heaven
Never seen him before
Only find out when I'm dead
Some believe, some don't
Time to find out if he's real
Is he real or is he not?
Calvin doesn't know

Haiku: I wonder...
Ho Yun Lee, Age 15

Illusions play eyes
Question what we really see
Is it all a trick?

Inspiration (Mother Teresa)
Amy Wates, Age 13

I may have feet,
But I was unable to speak,
Until she came.
I looked into her gleaming eyes
And the shadows on her face.
She outstretched her loving arms
And held me in her healing embrace,
She blows kisses of love and despair
To me and all.
She is the light of my candle,
The voice of my choir,
And now I have gained a new desire
To have such valour and love
And to be talented like she.
She is like a rare stone
Whom people adore.
Time walks on,
People alive or gone,
She was always there,
That is what I wanted to share.
She was valuable,
She was a princess
She was Mother Teresa.

Farewell old friend: Moving schools
Amandla Jarrett, Age 13

Time is late,
The sun has shone,
The boat has sailed,
The wind has blown,
Time in Graveney has been
As precious as a scarlet jewel.

Now as I begin to enter a new world
I realize how glorious walking
Through the ebony gates was.
How contented I felt
When playing on the green grass,
And how much pride and wisdom
I took in when my brain filled
With vital knowledge.

As a new door opens
Another one closes.
I await my fate filled with old memories.

I wonder: Gaia
Poppy Warner, Age 13

I wonder what it was like at the start,
When Gaia was a child.
She cared for us, gave us life,
We saw no poverty, no pollution, no strife.

I wonder what will happen
In the future far away.
Will Gaia become frail and old,
The tale of peaceful days unknown or untold?

I wonder what it is like now,
Backstage in the theatre.
Is Gaia on a torture rack,
As we search for coal, roughly breaking her back?

I wonder can we stop
The inevitable from happening,
Can we give our life giver
The chance not to wither?

You wonder why the natural disasters
Are repeatedly occurring.
Gaia sees the backstage shows
Yes my friends she knows!!

Peace: Dolphins
Rebekah Chaudery, Age 10

I wonder why we breathe
Nadia Al Refaie, Age 14

I've wondered for a while now
What makes us breathe
In and out

With languorous effort
Ambrosial air is acquired
Without second thought

Souls drown in ecstasy
As lungs seep in nothing
Invisible nourishment

An amazing process
Constant fabrication
In with the good
And out with the bad

Heads are comforted by pillows
But still the cycle goes on
Consciousness is done away with
And yet a breeze
Still moves the soul

I wonder ...
Nasira Karbhari, Age 14

If God visited you,
just for a day or two,
If he came unexpectedly,
I wonder: what would you do?
Oh I know you'd give your
Nicest room,
To such an honoured guest,
And you would surely serve him,
Your very, very best.

You would be your finest,
You're glad to have him there,
That serving him in your home,
Would be a joy without compare.

But when you hear he's coming,
Would you meet him at the door,
With your arms outstretched in welcome,
For your respected visitor?

And I wonder ...

If God spent a day
Or two with you,
Would you go on doing
The things that you always do?

Would you go right on saying
The things you say?
Would life for you continue,
As it does from day to day?

It might be interesting to know,
The things you'd really do,
If God came
To spend some time with you.

Deceptions
Joe Reynolds, Age 15

I wonder how the mind works,
Are we being deceived?
I wonder how our eyes work,
Are they just little thieves?

The peacock is a trickster,
He is actually brown,
What a strange creature,
He changes colour when the sun goes down.

Kitchener pointed out from the poster,
Always pointing at you,
Even when you go a little closer,
Your eyes deceive; he still stares at you.

I wonder about the universe,
Are we still in the dark?
Eyes aren't the beginning,
Our mind is where it starts.

Deep
Georgie Shipp, Age 17

When I was a child I asked someone of great wisdom
Who is God and where can I find him?
Is he in the sky?
The beauty of a new day breaking?

Is he the elegance
With which we dance, laugh, smile?
Is he in the sky
Or in the whispering trees?
Is he in me: in all the good I do?

I stopped.
I wondered.
I waited.
And then I thought …

If God is so amazing then why does he allow such disaster
     and despair?
Where is he when I need him?
Where are the angels when I need a lift?

I got angry …
Upset ….
And as a single tear fell down my cheek I saw it.
I saw the beauty,
And I realized
What I had missed all along …

He is always there,
In everything.
He is substance,
He is light,
He is love,
And he is good.

Disguised
Laura Tully, Age 17

You try and find the answer
though the question is not there
Locked inside the mind:
What's left? Happiness? Despair?
The scars erase, the cuts they heal
You struggle to recognize
Is this a phase? What do you feel?
Who is this in disguise?

Crystal memories mockingly shine
Reminding you of that place, that time
You see it all with a sinister sheen
Kodak thoughts for Kodak dreams
Climbing the floors you arrive at the sign
"You are here" but what did you climb?
The arrow it murmurs, aware of direction
The arrow it blurs: now where's your reflection?

You'll try and find the answer
Though the question is not there
'Trapped' inside the 'mind' you'll struggle
Living on this prayer
The scars erased, the cuts now healed
You'll finally recognize
There is no answer to this question
No truth to all these lies.

God is Everywhere
Caitlin Hynes, Age 13

Where is God?

Atheists say God's nowhere. Agnostics think he may be hiding. Feminists think he's a she. Believers – of many hues – may place the divine in the human heart, in the sacred space, in the running waves or in deep space.

Reflections from all points of view were welcome here. This was the most popular theme in the competition: the theological depth and beautifully chosen language of many of our young poets is breathtaking.

God is …
Chloe Crane, Age 6

God is as strong as a hundred leopards
God is as powerful as a storm
God is as strong as a T-Rex
God is as powerful as water
God is as big as the biggest pet
God is as powerful as a giant

Where is God?
Pedro Santos, Age 6

God is in love because the love is good.
God is in me because me is good.
God is in the underground because there is love.
God is in the tree because the trees have leaves.
God is in my heart because the heart is good.
God is all around because all around is good.
God is in my love because my love is all around.
God is in the animals I love because love is good.
God is in the best of friends.
God is in the heart of my heart.
God is everywhere.

Where is God?
Hamza Shafique, Age 7

God is everywhere
He is in different planets
Jupiter Saturn Venus
He can take life
Or give life
He is great
He never dies
Nobody is great as God

God is everywhere
Nicholas Martin, Age 8

God is where the sea meets the land
And where the land joins the sky
Where sky ends and storm starts
And where earth becomes space
God is everywhere

God is a runner
Jill Merlini, Age 7

God is a runner and a racer and fast.
God is a swimmer, fast and not last.
God is in heaven and air with the sky.
God is someone who seems to fly.
God is overhanging like a willow tree.
So if it rains he is a shelter for me.

God rhymes
Taylor Richardson, Age 7

Where is God?
God is in the flowers
Using his powers

Where is God?
God is in the cloud
Watching
Feeling proud

Where is God?
God is in the sun
Warming everyone

Where is God?
God is in the ground
Hearing every sound

Where is God?
Catherine Bridgewood, Age 8

God is everywhere
Up in heaven
down on the ground
God is everywhere

Even sitting next to me
And some more
where God can be
Cosy comfy in my bed
Me and God in my bed
Everywhere we go
God is there
Me and God
could not be pulled apart
But most of all
he's in my heart.

Where is God?
Elizabeth Thompson, Age 9

Where is God?
He's everywhere all around, in the air.
In the meow of a cat
And in the picnic spot where you sat.
He's in the sun which comes out every day
And in your voice when you say come and play.
He's in the highest mountain
And the smallest crumb.
He's in the good deeds of everyone.
He's in your heart and in your soul,
He's with you when you score that great goal.
Where is God?
He's easily found, just look around.

Where is God?
Lauren Hart, Age 9

Where is God?
He is in our lives
Everywhere we go
Rain forests and nature
Even in our words

In church
Souls and thoughts

God is in heaven
Our prayers
Deep, deep in us

God is everywhere
Chloe Beard, Age 10

God is the flow of the wind,
God is the beauty of the sunset,
The wave of the sea,
He is the scent of every flower,
The brightness of the ocean,
God is the highest of the sky,
God is the lowest of the ground,
He is inside every house,
The air that no-one sees,
God is in our minds,
God is in our favourite places,
God is everywhere!

Where is God?
Phillipa Beaumont, Age 10

Where is God?
In the bottom of
My heart where I love.
Where is God?
On the highest
Mountain where he listens to my dreams.
Where is God?
In the deepest
Ocean thinking of life and talking to me.
Where is God?
In space looking
Over a thousand stars.
Where is God?
In the forest of
Beauty loving you and me.
Where is God?
In a newborn baby every day.

I wonder, where is God?
Beth Schouten, Age 11

People in poverty
All God's fault
People drowning every day
All God's fault
Homes being sucked up in tornadoes
All God's fault

Birth and happiness
All thanks to God
Rainbows and happiness
All thanks to God
The universe and life
All thanks to God

God isn't anywhere
Edana Powell, Age 11

God is an illusion
And just in people's minds
I think that their imaginations
Are really running wild.

I think that the science
Is perfectly true
I believe we all evolved,
Every creature including me and you.

God is non-existent
And not at all around
I don't think he exists
Not on land in the sky or underground.

Science can almost prove that he isn't really there
And when the people go to church
They are praying to pure, thin, air
God isn't anywhere.

God as Colour
Sophie Ward, Age 10

Where is God?
Owen Davies, Age 12

Atheists
They believe in nothing, nothing at all,
So who's there to save them,
When they miss a step and fall?
Science they say,
Saves you from the grim.
Maybe they're right, there is no 'Him'.

Theists
They believe in God, Allah and Brahman.
They all say he saves you,
When you run out of friends.
But where is he when you're in a war?
Or praying for the life of your dying friend, where?
But maybe they're right, he's there,
When you need him most.

Agnostics
They don't know, and most don't care.
They don't know when, they don't know where.
Is he under the ground, or up in the air?
But should you fall ill (and there are so many ways)
Who will save you and keep you
Until the end of your days?

Maybe they're all right
Maybe he's only there
If you believe
And you want it enough.

Where is God?
Kathryn Beck, Age 10

Where is God?
I think he's in the air,
But you might think differently.

Where is God?
You might think he's in a church,
But I think differently.

Where is God?
He might think he's inside us,
But she might think differently.

Where is God?
She might think he's in heaven,
But he might think differently.

Where is God?
Where's God when the bad things happen?
Is God here at all?

Flutter of gold
Neilram Tanna, Age 12

Sunrise, daisies, foundations of blue,
Sapphires, pearls and rubies too.
Glittering gold, sensations of you?
This is what I wonder.

Sunset, roses, flutter from you.
Diamonds, opals and emeralds too.
Whispering, white sensations from you?
This is what I wonder.

I wonder, where is God?
Penny Barnes, Age 11

Is God out there?
Should I believe?

Things are confusing, is he alive
Has anyone seen him at all? Prove it
Everyone believes, but nobody knows
Reasons?
Everyone has one. But can

Anyone prove it?

God is real?
Or is he a myth?
Don't know, do you?
?

Where is God?
Amalie Bleackley, Age 12

Living in a marble mansion,
With golden gates
And plans for a pool expansion?
Lying on the dusty, baked desert floor,
Beaten by poverty, with hope no more.
Nested in the clouds (as many like to think),
With angels displaying plentiful bowls of grapes,
Each angel with a unique and charming wink.
Perhaps by a lake,
Reflecting on life, the world,
Maybe in a rainforest,
Studying each plant,
Its structure, how it curled.
Where is God?

Brahman
Martin Aitchison, Age 13

He is never seen
And never heard,
He's in a tree
And in a bird

He is the sun
He is the rain,
He is the happiness
He is the pain

He's with me through Samsara
And helps me with my Karma,
And until Moksha
He'll help me with my Dharma

With his help and guidance
I'll do the best I can,
Until we meet one day
Me and Brahman

Who are you, Brahman?
Yamba Katuka, Age 13

You are a butterfly and the mighty lion
You are the flowing river
You are the stone on every diamond ring
You are the plague that kills hundreds
You are the cure for an illness
You are the air in my lungs
You are the heat from the sun
You are the pain from a loss
And you are the joy from a gift
You are everywhere and everything
You are Brahman

Apple of Eden: after the event
Thomas White, Age 11

Colour flowing out like radiant waves,
The night time star awakening below.
As round as a ball, a small, thin pole my only life line.
Spots like freckles and juice like blood.
Juice flowing, swishing like the sea,
Juice exploding, my insides a blast.
My core shining like the sun,
Skin like leather, as smooth as a young child's skin.
The rusty insides where my lungs used to be,
Seeds raining from the soul.
Our souls as white as the moon above,
One crunch, another and that's the end.

What is God?
Sarah Billingsley, Age 13

What is God?
I don't know
Where is God?
I think I know

He's sitting in the garden
He's waiting in the street
He's inside the soul
Of everyone you meet

He's swimming in the ocean
He's flying in the air
He's standing in the doorway
He's lounging in the chair

He's running with the tigers
He's leaping with the frogs
He's sleeping with the lions
He's barking with the dogs

God is here
God is there
God is with us
Everywhere!

Where is God?
Abi Blaylock, Age 13

God's in the snowflake that melted
But not in the snowball you threw
She's in the midnight shadow that might
Have been there if the cloud only moved

God is in the words of the story
But not in the book's printed page
She's in every word that was shouted
But more in what you never dared say

God lives in the living fur's touch
But not in the leather punk boots
He is in the cool stars of midnight
But more in the dawn's golden fruits

God's in the first fair trade chocolate
But not in the millionth Kit-Kat
She's in the succulent pork meat
But more in Quorn. That's a fact!

God's not always in my heart
Or even in my head
But God can be there every step of the way
Even when he's just one step ahead

I am God
Jayne Perks, Age 13

I am the sun that shines for you,
I am the rain that rains for you,
I am the wind that blows for you.
I never ask for thanks, nor ever will.

I am the food that grows for you,
I am the drinks that are made for you,
I am the meat that died for you.
I never ask for thanks, nor ever will.

I am the stone that was cut for you,
I am the brick that was made for you,
I am the house that was built for you.
I never ask for thanks, nor ever will.

I am the life that lives for you,
I am the death that dies for you,
I am the morning and the evening star that shines for you.
I never ask for thanks, nor ever will.

I am the hope that was given to you,
I am the love that is in you,
I am the happiness that smiles on you.
I never ask for thanks, nor ever will.

Is God in pain?
Eloise Bowen, Age 13

Where is God?
Where was he when the bombers caused devastation in London?
Where is God?
Where was he when the twin towers collapsed?
Where is God?
Where is he when the soldiers get killed in Iraq?
Where is God?
Where was he when the floods and storms struck New Orleans?
Where is God?
Where is he when people are forcing children to take drugs?
Where is God?
Where is he when children are abused in their own homes?
Where is God?
Where is he when people are told they have terminal illnesses?
Where is God?
Where is he when people are hunting animals?
Where is God?
Where is he when people are chopping down trees in the
rainforest?
Where is God?
Where is he when mothers suffer miscarriages?
Where is God?
Where is he when young children are being bullied?
Where is God?
Where is he when young women are being raped?
Where is God?
Where is he when people are drawn to committing suicide?
Where is God?
Where was he when my Grandpa died and left my family broken
hearted?
WHERE ARE YOU NOW, GOD?

When the morning bird cries
Becky Bennett, Age 14

When the sun comes up over the hazy horizon in the morning
When the dew drops sprinkle their diamonds on the grass
When shades of blue paint their way across the dawn sky
And when the morning bird begins his cries
You will hear me

When the bees fly round the honeysuckle's sugar scent
When the wind spins and dances amongst your hair
When the grasses rustle and whisper around your ankles
And when the morning bird flies across the fields
You will hear me

When the sun burns its golden halo up high
When the maple leaves glisten on their branches
When water trickles and tumbles gently down a stream
And when the morning bird swoops down on its prey
You will hear me

When the soft rain drops like silk on your head
When the darting fox dashes over the hills
When the skies clap and the clouds rain down
And when the morning bird takes shelter from the rain
You will hear me

When the clouds clear their thunderous grey curtains
When the water drips from the gleaming trees
When the puddles evaporate up into the skies
And when the morning bird emerges safe from shelter
You will hear me

And you will hear me when the morning bird cries
For I am with you when the morning bird cries
And I am always walking with you
For you will hear me …

When the morning bird cries.

Brahman
Emma Rouse, Age 13

You are the sun
That's yellow in the sky
You make the choice
Whether we live or die

You are the creator
You start the circle
You bring health
And perform this miracle

You are the birds
That fly so high
You are the clouds
Fluffy and white

You bring the light and dark
And the moon up above
You bring sense and feelings
And also Love

Prayer of a dying atheist
Daisy Johnson, Age 14

Dear Nobody
I'm here
Judgement day arrived
And there's a few things I'd like to say
I wish I wasn't dying
Or praying
Or anywhere near this place
I wish that I was crying
So I could wash this cheap mascara off my face

I wish this bed was soaked
In all the blood you've supposedly wasted
I wish that I could tell them about the darkness
I wish I was an angel
With perfect paper thin wings
And beauty unmatched
By any one or any thing
But I never believed in that stuff

I wish I hadn't watched the news
Been a player in the awful, unimaginable game
I wish I had believed in you just once
So I could see what they all loved to see

So thank you God for proving me right
For showing me pain
And allowing no light
It means a lot to know I really was alone

And I believe I'm done
Have fun with creation

God?????
Jesse Cook, Age 15

If God was a her,
Would we praise her less?
Or would her breasts be
The object of our interest?

If God was a she
Would we believe?
Or would it more likely
Be Adam and Steve?

If God was a women
Would we bow down to thee?
Or would we respond with animosity?

If God was a goddess
Would our roles reverse?
And would men and women
Be so politically diverse?

I actually do wonder
If God was a her.

Where is God?
Luke Steven, Age 14

God is right here, everywhere, up there.
A triangle, a tricycle, a tripod.
God is that strange young man,
blue eyes, blonde hair
Who turns water into wine.
God is a bird, a pretty white bird
Who fills people up with fire.
God can often be seen
and sometimes heard
And is beyond the boundaries of time.

Where is God?
Bonnie Gifford, Age 15

I wonder, where is this so-called God of yours?
Where is he hiding, what is he hiding from us?
What good is an omnipotent God if he does not use his power
to help those who most need it?
What good is an omniscient God if he can see all, but do
nothing about it?
Where is this so-called benevolent God, when his followers,
when his believers, when his so-called children need him
the most?
What good is a God who lives in a sacred place, away from his
people, looking down at their need and suffering,
their prayers and pleas going unanswered?
What good is a God in the running waves of water, in the trees,
the air around us, when he as Mother Nature turns
against us,
Bringing floods and earthquakes in this flawed world he
entrusted us with?
What good is a God in the depths of space, detached from his
followers for all eternity?
Where is this God, if he even exists?
Some say he is in the human heart, that he and his spirit are
within each of his children, each of his followers.
Try telling that to the thousands starving each year,
to the millions dying of easily cured diseases,
To those who are homeless, to countries run by corrupt
politicians, to those living in poverty.
Where is your God now?
Try talking to those who have been reached,
who have been touched.
The homeless who have been given shelter and help,
those living in seemingly endless poverty who have been
saved by Christian Aid, by charities and private sponsored
projects.

Ask those who have lived on the brink, and have survived.
Those who lived in fear and pain and have still made it through.
Some will say God came to them, that he, surrounded by a
    bright light, brought about their salvation.
Wherever your so-called God is, there is a God, my God,
    in the hearts of all those who show kindness, support,
    love and care to those who need it the most, and receive it
    the least.
There is a God, or at least a part of him, in all our hearts.
It's just up to us whether we let him help us, and others, or not.

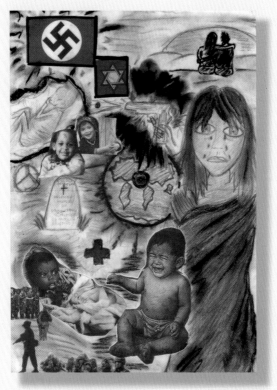

God in Good and Bad
Elena Hux, Age 15

Where is God?
I've got him
Jon Ord, Age 16

I have God tied up in my basement
I have tied him up using ordinary string
I have tied him to an ordinary chair
Doesn't seem so great now, does he?

Never mind why I have him.
If he got himself into this mess,
Don't you think a great lord could get out?

If you ever want to see God again
Send me £100 000 in an unmarked bag
Or alternatively
£5 a viewing
£10 a picture
£50 a punch!